G000017525

On Water

First published in 2014
The Dedalus Press
13 Moyclare Road
Baldoyle
Dublin 13
Ireland

www.dedaluspress.com

Editor: Pat Boran

ISBN 978 1 906614 92 8

Dedalus Press titles are represented in the UK by
Central Books, 99 Wallis Road, London E9 5LN
and in North America by Syracuse University Press, Inc.,
621 Skytop Road, Suite 110, Syracuse, New York 13244.

Printed in Ireland by Gemini International Ltd

Cover image Lovely Water No. 36 © Gary Coyle
www.garycoyle.ie

The Dedalus Press receives financial assistance from
The Arts Council / An Chomhairle Ealaíon

On Water

John O'Donnell

DEDALUS PRESS
DUBLIN, IRELAND

ACKNOWLEDGEMENTS

Grateful acknowledgement is due to the editors of the following publications where some of these poems, or versions of them, first appeared:

Agenda, BBC, The Bend, The Clifden Anthology, Cork Literary Review, Deep South (New Zealand), *If Ever You Go: A Map of Dublin in Poetry and Song* (eds. Pat Boran and Gerard Smyth), *The Irish Catullus* (ed. Ronan Sheehan), *The Irish Times, Looking For Orion, Our Shared Japan* (eds. Irene de Ingelis and Joseph Woods), *Oxfam Calendar, Poetry Ireland Review, Poetry On The Dart, RTÉ (Morning Ireland* and *Sunday Miscellany), September Sundays* (ed. Clíodhna Ní Anluain), *Something Beginning with P,* (ed. Seamus Cashman) *Southword, Stony Thursday, UCD RFC, Visions, The Watchful Heart* (ed. Joan McBreen) and *Wingspan: A Dedalus Sampler* (ed. Pat Boran).

Special thanks to Niall MacMonagle, all at 100 St Stephens Green, and the late Caroline Walsh for all their help in various ways.

CONTENTS

෴

I

II

for Michelene
and William, Jack, Eavan and Tom
who keep me afloat

I

Wilson

Years after all that, we're still out playing,
still together. I'm longer than him now;
now he complains his game is breaking down.
We both know what this means. Ahead, I wait

for him to make up ground between us, and grip
the club the way he showed, my thumb across
the maker's name: *Wilson*. Breathless
when he reaches me, he eyes my hands:

"You're holding on too tight." Is this
his way of saying goodbye or just bustle,
the golfer's artful chatter designed to unsettle?
Either way, it works: up close, where it matters,

he's all lobs and flops and lovely pitches, soft hands
that once saved the lives of stricken children
and still have what they call 'the touch'.
I stab and chop, the ball careening past the target,

first from one side, then the other while he
rolls his one sweetly up to stop. "Getting nearer,"
he consoles. The flag flutters above the cup
but I'm thinking of the other hole, the opened

ground where we'll all finish. His ball
just inches from the drop. Our lives together
a groove worn by my thumb. The *Wil* of Wilson
almost gone; soon all that will be left will be the *son*.

When Grumpy Met Lindy

Where I grew up they used to say
if you saw a car going round the streets
with no one driving it, that was him,

my grandfather. A pin-striped pocket battleship
patrolling the out-trays for forty years
in the Department, among the sniggerings

of nylons and Brylcreems who gave him the name
Grumpy, he only looked ahead and even now
would chide me for glancing over my shoulder,

feeling him close by as I go back
to 1936 when Charles A. Lindbergh,
'Lucky Lindy', came to Ireland for three days

and stayed for ten. A brown sea: hats at the aerodrome.
De Valera terrified, buttoned up for his first flight,
and Lindy, dapper in a suit and goggles, smiling

for the cameras, wondering when this November fog
would lift enough for him to head for home. Grumpy's
in a trilby, waiting in a line with the rest of the officials

to shake the hand of Lindbergh. His hand's outstretched,
the same hand that would later slip a coin for sums
well done or words spelt out correctly, that I might learn

the benefit of industry in addition to its virtue. Here
comes Lindy. The first man to fly the Atlantic
on his own! And I see the hand holding the stick,

head lifting up and up into the air until his grip
suddenly loosens, and my grandfather falls
beside his brand new walking-stick in our back garden

before I can discover what he'd said, if anything,
when they finally come face to face; a mumbled
greeting lost in clouds of breath, perhaps, or even just

the grin I'd settle for myself as I stretch out
my hand as far as it will go,
hoping I might touch a hero's wing.

Rare Birds

His hoard of shiny things the songs of others:
honeyeater, cockatoo and kookaburra
but less an artful thieving than a helpless ear
as now he sings out, innocent and exact

the whirr of camera-shutter, the rising grind
of chainsaws getting closer in rainforests of Australia
on the far side of the world, though nearer
than the southern seaside town we stayed in

every summer where my sister, aged thirteen
and already mad for road, spent all her days
loitering with intent amongst "the Willie boys",
Dillon and McCarthy, their arses worn away

from propping up street corners, and hit back
when taunted by me as to which one was her lover
saying I was nothing but "a langer", the Cork appendage
brandished by her in perfect sing-song pitch.

Carries his voice in a purse
clutched under his chin. Hunches
against distant thunder, rain

on the Masai Mara, a frock coat
on stilts, waiting for news
of the dead. A tree lifting into mid-air

is a dozen or more of them,
unbolting themselves
from the branches. Will hover

for hours above carrion
until lions are bloated, belching off
into the dusk; or loiter, the fringe

of a bush fire, as small scurries of feather
and fur leap safe from the flame,
to be snatched up and gobbled instead.

Cast out, snickered at by other,
brighter plumes, but never face
to face: the balding, blood-scabbed

head; the great blade of his bill
ready to cleave muscle and sinew,
to tear out a still-pumping heart

as night-time spreads its wings,
a darkness roosting
at the edge of dreams

or in the corner of a cage,
unrepentant as the day-trippers
pause to gape, and then move on

away from that steadfast
baleful stare, those eyes feasting
on the baby dozing in his pram.

North Carolina, 17.12.1903

Not far off freezing, wind
billowing over the flats,
sand stinging our eyes.
Too much, I thought, but he said
"No, just perfect," and gripped
my hand the same as always

though holding on a little longer
as if he knew. I lay down, could feel
her twitching underneath me —
muslin-flutter, flex of spruce;
on either side propeller-thrum,
the stink of gasoline —

and prayed *this time, this time,*
fingering the wire as she
warmed up, begun to trundle
down the tracks, and he was running
alongside, hollering "Yes, yes!"
my brother's cheers dying behind me
and below me as she lifted
into the beyond

for Eavan

So little time to teach you earth and air;
how hidden quarry shiver, your dark rumour
already scarifying as the cadgers
carry your wood cage upon their shoulders.
You're itching for the clouds as I untie
the jesses, lift the rufters. Blink of eye
and you are rising in an aria,
seeking perfect pitch, the stall before you
plummet, a dire judgement. Furious light,
you too will soon burn out: I am afraid
of bolt and shot, the poison laid in fields,
but more still of the day some young prince
comes a-calling, all smiles and easy charm
before he carries you away upon his arm.

Sleet

Not the big sister, trailing silently her elegant
white gown; nor the younger brother, impish,

a volley of pellets hurled at passers-by; nor
the eldest, long-prayed for and feared

who reigns in lyric mists, and sometimes
comes down hard; but the middle child,

a worry, neither one thing nor the other,
who's on his own, quietly making

a weapon he will one day use, the work-bench
weeping off-cuts, scraps of molten solder.

The Rifle

A wave of hand, munificent: "You'll have
one anyway." He pours; near-empty
bottle. 'Uncle' Jimmy. My father
settles back. My mother eyes the clock,
ushers us outside. A door opening to

a haggard, and waiting cousins, a firing squad
amused: our glass accents. Our city shoes among
the weeds, the mangled bones of some iron beast
that roamed the swaying fields beyond, a frontier
over which Jim-Bob stands sentry. A year on me

and more. I cannot tear my eyes off the weapon
he unshoulders for inspection. Barrel-sheen.
The pure white stock. The perfect sound the trigger
made when squeezed. And I would soon forget
the tears as we departed, my parents gently prising

the firearm from my grip, but not the long slim box
arriving just in time for Christmas, wrapped
in brown paper and twine tied up with whiskey fingers;
a brand new, pristine rifle, the same in every way
that I no longer wanted.

Roll Call

Andrews *whose pimples earned the nickname 'Pizzaface'*
Byrne *who left school early with two uniformed police*
Cosgrove *who rented out his brother's porno mags*
Daly *who sells pre-owned Beemers, Mercs and Jags*
Earley *who always wanted something more from life*
Farrell *who ran off with the history-teacher's wife*
Galvin (deceased) *who never learned to swim*
Hughes *who got five years for that pension investment scam*
Irwin *who in science class blew up a spotted toad*
Jackson *who blew up a crowded shop on the Kings' Road*
Kilroy *who carved his name on every single desk*
Lynch *who once at 4 am was dealt a Royal Straight Flush*
Malone *who despite everything turned out all right in the end*
Neilan *who still would sell his soul to have one friend*
O'Toole *who at the last count had fathered seven kids*
Power *who recently had the operation to become Ms.*
Quinn *who always hated any kind of football*
Reynolds *who so nearly won a bronze Olympic medal*
Sullivan *who would not believe what he could not see*
Tobin *who tested positive last week for HIV*
Usher *who, before he kicked it, drank away two pubs*
Valentine *who at his ninth attempt became captain of the golf club*
Wall *who was Head Boy and is now Third Sec in China*
Xavier *who was an altar boy and is now a Hare Krishna*
Young *whose antics in a pool brought down the Government*
Zee *who was then, is now, and always will be absent.*

The Clock Tower

Rung by rung we climbed, ascending into what seemed
a kind of heaven, the school's clock tower strictly out of bounds,
the pleasure in the lung-constricting terror, knowing the fall
would kill us. But we knew little else, and dying was so far off,
further than the dizzying football fields, the cars below like toys,
the matchbox houses lighting one by one the autumn evening,
and beyond all this the sea, clutching her frozen souls.
We were immortal then, untidy ink-stained gods
watching from on high, above time's granite certainties,
the steel hands of the clock-face like all schoolboys
never quite telling the truth, but set instead a little fast,
as if what lay ahead for us would not come soon enough.

XII

Clang of scaffolding
in icy light, the new year
going up brick by brick.

*

Letter-boxes bulge
with cards; the hospital waits
for a heart donor.

*

Blown out in a gale
discarded brollies, flapping
like exhausted bats.

*

Driving out to see
their only son at Easter:
fresh flowers for the grave.

*

Cherry blossoms strewn
outside the women's shelter.
Last year's confetti.

*

City packs a bag
heads off on a long weekend
wears its shortest skirt.

*

Street-glazzle, ooze of
tar. Spoke songs; ice-cream dripping
down a lobster arm.

*

Salty nights: damp hair
and skin, ears still full of sand
listening to the beach.

*

At the teacher's desk
a different face. The back row:
same old hand-me-downs.

*

Emptied cases. Cast
out on the side of the road
homeless chestnuts wait.

*

Scurry of small ghosts
house to house. Firecracker's trick:
echo of gunfire.

*

Thumped leather rising
high over the frosty pitch;
a muddy star.

Playmates

Under eaves adorned with Goldwing
and Led Zep, The Owls' First Team,
we gathered in grey flannel to thumb dog-eared
magazines that Suds' elder brother kept stashed
beneath the narrow unmade bed. So much there

for all of us to learn, our schoolbags
slingstones hurled below us as we thundered
up the stairs, a herd of hormones on stampede
to this top room. A window gave out onto the street
as we gave in to Playmates, Readers' Wives,

the curves and limbs of honeyed ladies awaiting
walnut-muscled men; and once, a gatefold
of two women embracing, naked, mouths shaped
in a perfect O as they moved in for the kiss. "Lezzers,"
proclaimed Donut, whose brother worked at weekends

in the European Film Club. The room swam.
We drowned for hours in dreams of glossy flesh
until we heard the song of Suds' Mum, Orpheus
in an apron, calling through the flames
of oven gas mark five for Suds to come down

for his tea. The door-latch clicked behind us
like an empty gun as we left, crossing towards the bus-stop
to begin the long fall home, girls in spring-green uniforms
cavorting round that maypole while we stood at a safe distance,
rooted, helpless as young trees, the sap rising, rising.

Easter Island

My mother lit the lamp beside the statue of Our Lady,
her knees stiffening in the month of May
as she begged us say the Rosary each night, and I
would nudge my giggling little sister and recite

the joyful mysteries we learned on summer voyages:
Baily, Fastnet, Tuskar, Hook, Old Head as we sailed
on leaky boats, a not-so-Holy Family, waving as we passed
to those keepers of the light patrolling the murette who always,

always would wave back. I grew up. I read in books
how many souls those cheery men had saved, and
learned as well how hard it was to place my faith in one who
        claimed to be
The Light but who only looked on as crops failed and planes

fell from the sky, who would allow the lump within
my sister's breast to bloom. We waited for a sign, news
from the hospital, my mother on her knees once more,
lighting candle after candle, the nave ablaze with flame

in a church that now was empty. Once, during the chemo,
I saw her lift off her bandana, and shuddered at the terror
of her head laid bare. I thought of Easter Island,
its lonely shore named for the promise of an after-life

by other sailors who'd also lost their way and could not believe
the brute heads looming over them as they beached rowboats
on the sand, stone deities they could not account for
as they wondered what they might find next, and were afraid.

27

Amendoeira

I love this story my mother told me:
the Moorish prince who falls in love
and marries a girl from the far North.
He brings her home. The palace marvels:
her skin of ivory, her wheaten hair; her slivers
of sapphire streaming sadness. She misses
her own home, and most of all she misses
snow. And so, because he loves her and cannot
bear to see her cry, the worried prince commands
that every field be planted with amendoeira,

trees of almond blossom. The young princess
shrugs, resumes her bathing in the pool
of her own misery, hating the scent of musk,
the rustling silks, the fat-faced watchful maids.
A season passes, and another, and then early
on a breezy day in spring the prince bids
his heart-sore princess come to the window
that she may see the snow his love has made
for her, a blizzard of pink blooms falling
across the land. And here the story ends

or should do: the princess weeping, this time
with joy; the prince beside her gazing proudly
at the laden boughs. But what happens next,
I want to ask: how does love survive the empty
limbs, the fleshy drifts becoming rust?
And then my mother brings me to the window,
pointing to the tree planted so long ago,
the tree my own children are shrieking under now,
hurling armfuls of blossoms at each other,
and my father, still shaking the branches.

Hoppers

Jeez your hands are freezing, she'd said more than once,
his big paws struggling to hold her as she squirmed
beneath him, this gleaming silver prize
he'd scooped out of the water,

one we always knew would get away, escape
the fish-tin jongling down the street, tied to
the Just-Married car we'd waved off at the hotel,
and gathered round again, as sweating rescue-workers

hauled dripping metal from the river and tried to prise
the locked doors open. Two the pine, but ten to raise
the oak, she following down the aisle behind the coffins
in tight new widow's weeds. *His greatest ever catch,*

the best man had said, to laughter; her, and the tiddler
son they'd landed a year later. He'd taught that boy
the pitch and flick of casting, how to watch for stirrings
on the rod, and how to bait the line with hoppers

captured in long grass, buzz and scurry in an airless jar,
clarets, ambers, pearlies, pierced to hide the hook;
how beauty at first tempts and then reveals its barbed surprise.
And how to wait, drowsy by the river, dreaming

of tight lines, or sleepless under night skies filled
with planes he'd thought were stars, awaiting her return
from far upriver, spawning elsewhere with another,
glitter of her still-damp scales, and tears when she'd said

she wanted out. But he'd reeled big ones in before,
ones looking to escape the net; all it took was patience,
he told himself, loading carefully the car for the last time,
rods and reels stashed in beside the anxious child;

patience, and the right bait. *Accidental,* the coroner declared,
though the road straight and the bridge across the river wide;
and why anyway, why, unless that slow arc of the car through
    air
his final cast, offering to the river his firstborn,

like ancients desperate for a fair harvest or rain, as if
love were a greedy fish unable to resist the lure strapped
into the back seat, rising open-jawed from reed-choked gloom
to snatch away this life, so short, so bright, so sweet.

Winter Moon

for William Crozier

We must have missed a sign
along the way, or taken a wrong turn
that turned out right. Here is a new road
arcing towards the sea, past fields ablaze
with sulphur, haystacks looming indigo
in the last of evening. Headlands wear
magenta to honour sunset, and out among
the jazz of waves a crimson island

rises, far-off wedge of cake.
We stop. Unfolded map. Heads bent,
we pore, trying to find where we are
and where we should be headed. Our windows
mist: first frost. Something else is also
peering in, high on the driver's side;
early bloom of moon, spotlighting
this silent road, this solitary tree,

arms outstretched now to greet
the night sky's winter apple, where
all things lost on earth are treasured:
our prayers, unanswered yet.
Our broken vows. And soon
this moment's gleam, before we turn the car
and go back where we came from,
our headlights on, burrowing into the dark.

Corner

Something in the corner of your eye,
ditch-edge, a small bright blur
you almost miss, glanced at, going by

and then a second time, momentary
distraction from the road ahead, wheel-whirr;
something on the corner. And you eye

the fresh bouquet. Somebody will tie
another here tomorrow, the day after;
someone who'll never miss a chance, going by

this asphalt curve to stop, to wonder why
he hadn't stopped in time, the driver
who'd seen something in the corner of his eye

before he'd braked, the screeching geometry
of one life arcing to avoid another
and almost missing, bumper's glance going by

and now no going back. You straighten, lonely:
how this sudden turn becomes a tear
somewhere, in the corner of an eye,
a loved one missed; a chance gone by.

The Dive

We plough the water, idle over coral,
heads bowed to glimpse the promised shoals of colour
hidden down near caskets stuffed with treasure
lost since childhood. What we search for still
eludes us. Sunlight, shadow; my son's skin
mottles beside me, and his grandfather swims
lithe into my head, all glistening abs and pecs,
girls screeching as he dives off summer rocks
and disappears, comes up again years later,
more than ocean in between us. Now I wear
a father's wheezy snorkel, rheumy mask:
this boy next me dreams of sweetlip, rainbow wrasse,
an angelfish in flower, sudden bloom before my eyes.
His fin brushing my arm. And then he dives.

Poetry

for Conor O'Callaghan

The dark nights at the driving range.
The early starts, sun singing off the dew.
The shudder, standing up to open ground
On the first tee. The many ways of being wrong:
Hooked. Sliced. Topped. Shanked. Pulled.
The floundering for hours in bunkers
And still not getting out. The lost balls.
The prizes everyone else wins. The drinking.
The yardage, working out how far to go.
The ones that start off looking great but end up
Short. The shots that try to do too much. The know-alls.
The two-foot putts that you still miss. The yips.
And — sometimes — the little click when things go right:
The sweet sound that keeps you coming back.

II

Two Team Sheets

I THE NIGHT BEFORE

House full of whiskey and ruby-faced men
who'd played there themselves, or nearly played once

up for the match and in need of a bed
way past my bedtime, blue plume of Silk Cut

and the airs of old songs drifting upstairs
staying on the next day, though the windows

thrown wide, not wanting to leave, a shy guest
in the corner long after the others

now gone to the ground, ghosts back here tonight
to gather me up in folds of damp tweed.

One joker up on tiptoe at the back;
centre, the proud captain, holding ball. Arms
folded in a swagger, we were ready

for anything the world could hurl at us.
Pirate beards, teen-idol hair — the glamour:
we were sure to knock 'em dead

in the bar after. Boots crusting with pitch-muck
and tradition; the jerseys that on fired-up afternoons
we'd sworn we'd die for. And (not in picture)

the all-in-this-together of it, lingering here
like the reek of Deep Heat in the changing-room
as players take the field to scattered cheers.

Dún An Óir

The head settles on the pint
just pulled by Mrs Quinn
as 'Gooch' Cooper, rust-haired, *gamine*
— think young Cate Blanchett, as the Virgin Queen —
from thirty yards out knocks a point
over the bar. Three in it. "Game on!"
shouts someone, but on the radio
Weeshie Fogarty is praying for a goal,
a Pape soldier on his knees at Dún an Óir
pleading in Italian to be spared, cries
lost to surf-boom, screech of gull;
his throat sliced open, Lord Grey's
blade. The final whistle; ball goes wide.
Six hundred of them, lolling on the tide.

Shakespeare in Ireland

One bearded me, hop-addled, the hour late;
a rug-haired kerne, grog-blossoms in full bloom.
"What business have you here?" The age-old hate
glittering in those bane-filled eyes; the room
full suddenly of music, flute and fiddle,
as snag-toothed locals gaily take the floor,
advance, retreat, advance, rehearsing battle;
a merry dance they led us. But what for?
A charnel-house, this place: rain-lashed, hag-cursed,
a song that's sung shut-eyed against the pain.
There is no future here, only the past;
a blood-revenant, come to avenge the slain,
who'd this night gladly kill me, one brute blow
as jigs and reels come rivering off the bow.

Beads

When the wire-ends pricked our fingers the sisters
urged we think of Jesus, and how little was our suffering
by comparison. We threaded bead on bead to make
a decade at a time of our time here, ten years gone
along with songs we sang in choir, as if
our soaring voices could lift us also upwards
to that other world from where the swan had come
crash-landing in the yard, off-course, beautiful and stunned
before taking fright and taking off again, wings
still beating in our ugly-duckling hearts. We made
Our Fathers and Hail Marys, Glory Bs and wondered
where our own mothers might be, and what we had
done wrong to end up here, standing in a line
on freezing mornings, our sodden bed-sheets
draped over our heads, unholy ghosts who saw
through tear-scald and the wet stench of ammonia
the other, darker stains of older girls
and were afraid of where we next would bleed.

Skellig

The night the Abbot died all the book-satchels
fell down, their psalters scattered over the stone floor
like ransacked towns. I could feel Flann's bony knee

pressed close, too close to mine as we gathered in to pray,
the oratory an upturned boat, and we twelve souls the crew,
marooned out on this rock. *"Never can we hide*

from the Divine," intoned the doleful Malachy, already bristling;
the importance of new office. I bowed my head and wondered
if He could see the claw of Flann's right hand, rummaging

underneath his habit, or how Aodh quaffed as always
a little too much wine from the battered chalice. Outside stone
     huts
huddled in the gale, two rows of rough-cut crosses in the
     graveyard

a mouth of broken teeth as we prepared the body, muttered
supplications to forgive the dead man's sins. Will He also
forgive Fionan, prayers on sunny days forgotten as he dozes

amongst sea-pinks and the daisies; or vain Cellach in the
     garden,
swagger of the hoe he handles better than any other man;
or Aeneas, swearing by the names of all the saints

that this portly sad-eyed puffin trembling in his hands
was really more fish than fowl, whose flesh we thus
could safely eat on Fridays? And will He also forgive

other carnal pleasures? Before this, back on land,
bells tolled as monks warned of the devil's many forms;
how the young girl I'd watched working in the scullery

could be the shape of evil. Head down, pert rump up,
her hands were small birds fluttering among the tunics
and the scapulars. One loosened strand of hair dangled

from her cap like a dark question. "You have answered
the call of God," the elders rasped, "who asks you serve him
somewhere else instead, away from all temptation." Now I

lay down my days in dry stone walls, and kneel on clouds
to set into the cliff the steps we build, rising from the cove,
each slab a prayer ascending into heaven. We plant

celery and parsnips, and stake our faith in this high place;
no frost or plague can reach us, and even the bravest longship
fears to cross these widow waves. I know the cry

of kittiwake and razorbill, the time of every tide,
and on clear days can see south to the Bull Rock, and the Cow,
but know as well I'll never see again that little maid

who comes to me in dreams in my dark cell. Some night
I'll stiffen in my sleep for the last time. And then? And then?
The greatest sin of all the sin of doubt: that all there is

is all we leave behind; crude annals, the sound
of callused hands working stone. *Matins. Lauds.* We count
the hours on knotted cords, keep vigil for gentle Muredach

until dawn, pink light blooming on the arch
of Needle's Eye and on the stations, a *via Crucis*
hewn from wind and rock. I'll offer up

these blistered fingers aching for fond caress,
and press my lips instead against this wooden cross,
praying that my sins may fall from me like tears.

The Volta

Ireland's first cinema, opened in 1909 by James Joyce

A gleam, this new idea in his head:
a chance of turning coin, his city still
in blackness, awaiting sound and light

so he comes back, acquires a hall
off Sackville and fills it; wooden
benches, Windsor chairs for the quality

a carpet sticking its red tongue out
along the centre aisle, potted palms
beside the orchestra, and a screen

and opens in December, frost and ice
and snow that soon would be
general all over Ireland

counting heads, the queue outside
curious under gaslight;
then curses the bad weather as the stream

dries to a trickle, the money
running out, and closes six months later
the doors locked and the posters

gone, but not the taste for it.
How well he knew us
as we crowd in once again

loving the womb-warm inky dark,
the press of flesh, and stories stories
stories created out of all of us, pictures

alive in flame-flicker, a huddle around
cave paintings made from the crushed
bones and blood of the animals we painted.

Dick The Younger

As a boy he lured strays into the yard
with purloined titbits of offal they all fell for,
the condemned mongrels struggling to escape

as the cord tightened on the gibbet Johnny Appleseed
had sworn he'd seen him making, though Mary Parr
was doubtful, and Ellen Cooper shook her head of wheat

saying it had been fashioned by his father, who
like his son had one cast eye, as if a part of him
could not bear witness to the dark art of his office,

an heirloom grimly handed down. Though crops failed
his tree bloomed all year round, dangling
from its single branch our whole town's rotten fruit,

utterers and cutthroats, murderers and highwaymen
we'd thrill to watch being hoist, their boots kicking the air
in a last polka: 'Sweet' William Webster, who stole a ewe,

grinning his idiot grin as he slowly climbed the scaffold,
and Widow Howcroft, who poisoned seven babies,
screeching obscenities in the shadow of the rope,

the knot that Dick The Elder had learned from his own father,
who'd likewise grumbled at the cost of ladders, and had known
in a handshake a felon's counterweight; thirteen hitches,

and an eye the rich and poor could pass through. That winter
the fever came for Mary, the Divine Lord deciding
fourteen summers was enough, and in the springtime

Dick The Younger came for me, clutching shyly
a posy of snowdrops, the blooms already dead. "As well him
as another," my mother said, who worried I was plain,

though I'd have chosen Johnny Appleseed, by whom Ellen
bore ten children. And I bore one: this wall-eyed child cradled
beside me,who in time will learn to bargain with the Crown

over expenses, who soon will set our sinners dancing
to his tune, and whose small fist closing tight around
my finger may yet weigh me for the drop.

Owel

Nightwing, a shadow moving among trees,
echoing the name for these dark waters
in the middle of the island. And here is Malachy's
only daughter, peace-offering from the old king

to the new: Turgesius, his kingdom come
by oar and sail. Hit and run. The dane-geld levied
and a prey of women taken. Tonight his bloodshot eyes
are feasting on the folds of her garments,

his courtiers banished to the camp, her ladies
demure, standing off as he moves in, a frenzy
of blistered hands. She sighs, leans back, her haunches
opening to his staff, knowing his head's gone,

blood pumping to the muscle; knowing he can't see
the Adam's apple bobbling like an extra vowel
in the throats of those unlovely maids-in-waiting
now unsheathing their own swords from underneath

ill-fitting skirts to surround Turgesius, his britches
round his ankles, moonlight on their blades. Malachy
steps forward, still comic in a dress as he reclaims
his shaken daughter, and more. Here is the sound

of vengeance, dying splashes of the raider as he slips
beneath the surface of this place, the lake a loyal servant
who keeps secrets down deep, among the brown trout
and the sedge. Who sees everything. And waits.

Kecksies

"As good as any lad"; my father, swallowing, anxious for
the stranger's shilling. *"She'll do."* I walked behind him from the
    market
as he pointed with his ashplant to fences and the river,
and swollen-uddered cattle in the pasture, waiting. His wife's eyes
on my hips as she led me to the milking-shed, and I knew
she was a field no seed would grow in. The beasts came easy
as I squeezed the way my late mother had shown. Churns

filled: a bumper yield. He came easy too, when we lay down
amid the lowing and the shuffling of hooves. My belly swelled.
He promised me the top field, the smallest cow, but one night I
heard her soused, asking him where I'd go once they'd got the
baby,
and he tapped the ashplant and said river. My mother showed
    me
something else as well: how to find them in the ditches,
    amongst
docks and thistles, the white flower and rank leaves which
    meant

the bad seeds she called kecksies. Next day I tied the little heifer
and drove the others to the river, watching as they tumbled
    ullulluing
into the dark water. I laced each brimming churn, and seasoned
with those husks a parsnip sauce for supper, imagining them both
suddenly struck dumb among the dishes, their bodies slumped
like sated children in their chairs. On the road I whispered to
    the heifer
and listened to the grass in the top field. Inside the kecksie
    stirred.

Zippo

The young man on Hang Gai selling Zippos
is the same age as the soldier he claims left this behind
during the war. "American," he says, urging I admire

the polished casing and insignia, the bleak inscription
when I die I'm going to heaven I've already been
in hell. He flicks the cap and thumbs the wheel

and a small flame comes to life on this street corner,
enough to light a teenage Lucky Strike, or set ablaze
a roof of thatch, enough to see the blood spurt from

his sudden wound, a thousand eyes around him, watching
in the dark. He shuts the cap. We both know this
is fake; we both know this artifice of brass and petrol

was fashioned in a backroom by nimble-fingered children
born long after the last rotor, the sons and daughters
of other soldiers who laid traps and planted mines

and promised never to surrender until the enemy were gone,
flown home in body-bags, the dog-tags handed over
but not the lighter a young girl snatches from the mattress

she'd shared briefly with that boy, if not for love
then for something both were happy to pretend was
almost the real thing, this girl who carries now inside

the child he never lives to see. "American," she says, pointing
to her belly in the queue at Immigration, and holding out
the Zippo for inspection as she waits to enter his country.

The Artist and his Mother

after Arshile Gorky

Here is a picture of the artist
and his mother. On the left,
the artist; me. On the right my mother;

your wife. But you know all of this
already. See how respectfully I stand,
feet together, my good coat buttoned up,

my right hand holding a posy I have gathered
from the apron of my mother who sits
beside me, staring out at you. I am eight years old

and you are in America, avoiding the army call-up here,
promising to return soon to where this is taken:
Van, Armenia. 1912. Hold the picture

closer. Do you see the smashed-in doors
of emptied houses, the streets strewn
with corpses, a people on the march

at gunpoint to the work-camps and the borders,
their bags crammed with heirlooms and heartbreak?
My mother stands. She gives a coin

to the photographer. Eyes closed, I press my face
once more into her apron, inhaling the stitched flowers,
the patterns I will embroider in her memory

my whole life. Can you smell her death
a few years after this photograph is taken:
sparrow-light, exiled in Russia, starving,

broken down by loss of country, loss of husband?
We post this off so you may not forget us.
I imagine an early morning in America,

sun on stone, the chirruping of redwings
as the mail arrives, your hands opening
the envelope; I see all of this, but never see

your new wife, younger, prettier,
busy in the next room. You hide the photograph,
stuff it deep into the darkness of a drawer

where family secrets are always kept, this picture
of a life you have left behind, a wife and son,
chief mourners at the funeral of a marriage;

she seated, me standing beside her,
the last passengers waiting on a platform
in a station where the train no longer comes.

Lamp

i.m. Caroline Walsh

Before cave-paintings there were caves,
wretched places, cold and damp and dark,
and although they built fires at the entrance,
and gathered round in skins to eat the burnt flesh
of slain deer, and kept watch for sabre-tooths
and ravenous bears prowling the ice wastes,

they were afraid to look behind, back
past the shadows into the blackness
of the deepest reaches of those walls
where no one dared to go without a light,
and all those bulls and stags and horses
would have stayed inside the small brains
of the hunters unless one of the tribe

had not taken a sandstone slab, and slowly
hollowed out in it a space for deer-fat
and a sprig of juniper as a wick, and kept it lit
so that the painters, and the others,
could see what they were making;
fabulous beasts, whinnying and prancing
and pawing the ground, alive
in the guttering flame of a careful lamp.

Last Orders

I. One For The Road

i.m. Gregory Murphy

I'm choosing (you'd love this) a tie to wear
in Foxy John Moriarty's, the best shop
in West Kerry for getting kitted out
for a funeral. Whether you'd approve
of what I've at last selected, I doubt:
I'm almost sorry for The Man Above
as you arrive, grumbling about standards dropped;
how these days they'll let anyone in here.
Still, it could be worse. I'm certain you won't fail
to find some smoke-filled corner to regale
with scandal, gossip, good-humoured attacks
on petty vanities, delight in getting people's backs up
and putting — in defence — the odd good word
since your cloak sheltered many a wounded bird.
So keep a space for me, as I keep you in mind
knowing there's no filling the space you've left behind.

i.m. Eamon Leahy

Perhaps the afterlife will be a table
set with candles, silver, long-stem glasses
in a restaurant where we'll all meet up,
sit down again together for a long and boozy

lunch. I fancy I can hear you celebrating
with a couple of the others who got there
so much earlier than we'd thought, telling stories
about half-mad beaks and hacks, Party men,

chancers that you've met, laughter filling
the whole place, the waiters pumping sweat
as they ferry in more food and wine. They'll earn
their overtime; this could go on all night.

And though it's hard right now to eat, a lump
in every throat since an unexpected gust
just blew the brightest candle out, I'll drink
a toast instead, if you don't mind — as if you would,

O happy Buddha: your big smile. And bigger heart.
To you I raise the biggest glass that I can find.

III THE UPSTAIRS BAR

i.m. Paddy Hunt

After we've searched all the usual haunts
someone suggests we try The Upstairs Bar,
a new place, on the main street, sandwiched between
a chi-chi restaurant and a wound-down video store

in this village where you've long time been
the unelected mayor, and here you are, practising as ever
the art of conversation, thrust and parry, to and fro,
and all the while an ear cocked and a weather eye

for nuggets of gossip, tittle-tattle to add to your collection,
gems you'd feign at first a pantomime reluctance to show us
before relenting, dropping gleefully each bright new stone
into the pool, then sitting back to watch the ripples spread,

and so much else stored up there, in the attic of this house
we close the door and turn the key on; tax wheezes and the tunes
of all the songs, the last word on everything and a word
for everyone, the mighty and especially the fallen,

willing to go a bit of any road except the road for home,
and a place too in your shy heart for children, who sensed
your sense of mischief that would surely have had you
sniggering with delight in the course of your own funeral

at the stern warnings from the pulpit on the evils
of double-parking in church grounds, and the delicious,
knowing praise of your "support for local industry" delivered
to pews filled with long-faced barmen, the queue of sympathisers

stretching back to Cork and Sligo, the length and breadth
of this island which seemed sometimes too small for you,
the air hostesses three parts charmed, one part bemused
as you sipped lethal gin and tonics the whole flight,

and if the Buddhists have it right maybe you'll fly back
one day as a parrot, landing on the shoulder of a clutch
of balding legal eagles and other quare hawks, where you'll
squawk once more in protest at their feeble-minded drivel,

but if it's The Upstairs Bar instead it'll be a fine place
to walk into and find you, soaking up the atmosphere,
as you turn with a smirk, and a quick rub of the beak to say
glint-eyed, conspiratorial, *"I shouldn't be saying this ..."*

III

Raindrop

This you know: the muffled drumbeat
singling out your window, diamond
on the glass; or, from a sullen cloud
a pearl on your lapel dissolving, a dark wound.

Now look again: this cradling of light
suspended from the edge of leaf is like
the swaddled infant dangling from the beak
of the stork that brought new babies when we

were young and could not understand.
One last time, while there's still time to see
me and you, the garden where we stand,
our world shrunk to this gleam

the slightest shudder would let fall.
Into a cupped hand which may not be there at all.

The Pinnace

after Catullus

See her? Once she was the fastest
of the fleet; oar or canvas, Adriatic
to Aegean, there was nothing on the water
that could touch her. But you knew this,

since she grew up on these green slopes;
leaf-whisperings on Mount Cytorus, a forest
hewn, bark becoming bark. And such
a sturdy craft: from when her blades

first dipped in the blue waters off Amastris
there were no winds she couldn't trim to,
no seas she couldn't handle, close-hauled
on port or starboard, clipping over the waves

or downwind under thunder-clouds, the gale
a howling god. No need to pray she'd hold
her course off a lee shore; on ocean's swell
or lake of glass, she was as constant

as the lights she steered by, coming home.
Tonight she thanks those lucky stars again,
this time the last. Her voyage over; this berth
the end. All things must pass.

The Lusitania

Hiss of grill: would scratch your eyes out. We kept
our distance at the counter as we waited
for charred glories served by Jonjo, burger-
meister, furnace-faced and blowing like a stoker
from the ship he'd named this shack for, torpedoed
in an earlier war. Behind me, stifled giggles;
my younger sister, thirteen, treacherous,
her best friend B.J., who'd taken on new cargo —
last year *The Bunty*, this year Bardot —
winking back at Jonjo as he handed out
the baps. We licked our chops, prepared to eat
our hearts out, wounds spurting ketchup unto death
in ancient grease: one love-sick glance, another fleet
sailing for Troy, on gusts of onion breath.

What They Carried

Sometimes a brimming trunk lugged miles
past smashed-in cabins, empty rills, ditches
clotted with the dead, but mostly
a life bundled in a blanket;
gansies, shawls, a pot and spoon,
a bauble for the baby not yet born

or whatever they stood up in,
darned petticoats and fraying trousers,
a hat jammed on a head teeming
with dreams and busy lice, the typhus
travelling with them to the fever shed
at King Street, the lazy beds of Cabbagetown

dozens buried at a time, their last rite
a shovelful of lime. They braced themselves
against the lurch of ocean and the future
and vowed to keep the faith they'd never lost,
despite all this, in a merciful Almighty
who watched them as they clambered up
through narrow hatches, down on to the dock
to stand shivering, exhausted in new light;

who listened always, they insisted,
to their whispered supplications
that what they carried with them
might be equal to these streets
already greening to new leaf
and what they'd left behind
or thought they had. Clay
under their fingernails. Their grief.

Noor's Pigeons

Incense. Mutton curry. Whiff of sweet illicit dagga
and cheap perfume, the working girls on Russell and Hanover

street-names naming more than streets, Smart Lane and Rotten Row.
Glee and clatter of the markets, and the stomp and jazzy blow

of music on the breeze, notes hanging alongside washing
and wingbeats over rooftops, Noor's pigeons returning

as his wife tries on a new one down at De Nova Hats
on the never-never, what you has you has, before the Acts:

the envelopes arriving in a flurry of brown snow
that tells you what you are and the date you are to go

to Manenberg. Nyanga. Khayelitsha. Gugulethu.
The new townships, home now where they send you in a letter

the loft on Caledon dismantled, his birds caged for the journey
as signs go up on every wall: "Slegs Blankes" Whites Only,

heartbeats thrumming against bars, sweep of wind under the Table
to the sands of the Cape Flats, dust and cardboard and scrap-metal

where Noor builds a kind of loft, and a kind of life as well
and three months later sets them free, lump in his throat the swell

of envy, knowing if he'd wings he too would soon be gone
an arc over the city towards Hanover and Caledon

those loved familiar streets now gone as well, only the pull
within hauling him back here to perch atop the rubble

of what was lost; the place inside he'd thought he'd always own,
a scattering of feathers on hot tar the word for home.

On Water

(i) A WEDDING GUEST

We stayed just outside Cana, which is actually
a very pretty town, although the military
seemed to be everywhere. The weather on the day
was perfect — I wore my new papyrus shoes —
and the bride looked absolutely radiant
(her dress cost a small fortune). They did choose
to serve the best wine last, after a slight delay
but the customs they have here are different,
as Zach explained. Still, it did seem rather odd,
as did that young man (the woman by his side
his mother, I believe) who spoke to the stewards;
so quiet and assured as they fussed over the ewers.
The group with him were whispering about a sign:
a rough lot, they were. But the wine tasted divine.

(ii) The Basket

I heard them mutter as they counted heads
that this was madness, how there'd never be
enough even to go around themselves,
never mind the rest of us. We could see
the darkness rolling over the sand
and huddled close together, watching him.
A dog barked. A child who could not understand
her hunger cried. I thought again of home,
so far away, so many of us here
with so little to go on. Then the voice,
his murmured blessings rising in the air,
rustles as the wicker passed along. My hands
plunged in: warm bread; fish-scales, the tang of sea.
The basket was as deep as Galilee.

(iii) THE STORM

We should have seen it coming, I suppose,
but we were dog-tired when we left, and skies
seemed clear, the sun's work done, sinking astern.
He'd flaked out down below, missing his turn
to steer — and who could blame him, wanting peace
from days of heat and dust, and everywhere
excited hordes, clamouring for a piece
of him. A shame to wake him, but we were
in real trouble, too late to shorten sail,
heaving waves swamping the decks, the boom of gale
enough to raise the dead. I slapped his face:
"We're going down! Don't you care?" He blinked, then stared
as if he'd come back from another place
to wind and water, waiting for his word.

(iv) BAPTIST

But no one knew from where. Feral, hairy,
his beard alive with insects, streaks of honey;
that stinking hide! And wounded, wounding eyes
urging repentance on the restless queues
as we lined up to take the plunge. Hawkers
selling song-birds, dates and sherbets; raucous
warnings of sandal-thongs, the everlasting fire
until they met. Awe, perhaps, or fear;
his voice a quiver as he beckoned him wade out
to where he stood. Hands cupped over the bowed
head; a river falling through his fingers. Dove?
No. No voice; no heavens opening above
except after: rain, long prayed for, from blue skies
like sudden small clear blessings on our lives.

(v) JAIRUS

One with him shook his head: *"You can't buy this"* —
although I could see the other two were
keen to haggle, see how much more I'd give,
as if there was some price I would not pay
to bring her back. To see my daughter live.
A swarm around him, pawing at his robes
and he was weary, wheeling with a sigh
"Alright; alright." Dark room; her husk. Choked sobs
when he pronounced her sleeping, urging her
to rise. The same as all the rest, I thought:
the rhetoric, the empty promises;
I'd *wanted* to believe, you understand,
as he called for water. The cup lifted
to lifeless lips. And then she touched his hand.

(vi) ON WATER

I'd seen it happen years ago, back when
he was just a child; couldn't have been more
than eight. I'd warned him: stay close to the shore,
don't go deeper than your knees. But even then
he had this way of doing what he thought was right.
My back was turned — his baby sister, red-cheeked
in the heat — and he was gone. I panicked;
ran down to the edge, screamed his name in fright
until I saw him, going out with the tide
walking on water. Little splashes as
he skipped from wave to wave; astonished fishes
leaping underneath his feet. Arms stretched wide,
he smiled back, showing how easily it was done.
Which it was, compared with what was yet to come.

IV

The Queen of Calabar

"Dashee," says the caboceer,
"first you pay me dashee

then I bring you best of men;
best of women too." He laughs,

clutches his stalk, and then
the browfow laughs, and clutches

his own stalk as well, staring at us,
counting, his one good eye a blade

and rows us out, a little boat
so full it almost tips, to where

the ship stands, named in gold
The Queen of Calabar. They carry

firesticks and whips; they carry
coils of sleeping chain to tether us

down here, a darkness darker
than the darkest cantsee. So

many of us: small jariri screaming
as they cling on to their mamas,

wild-eyed shouting men, and younger
men as well; I can hear the voice of Hadi,

thirteeen also, who kissed me once
beneath the branches of the acacia

calling out my name and promising
that soon we will be free. Our lives

tilting in the airless, stinking dark
though sometimes the roof opens, a rain

of yams and plantains, gobbagobs
we scrabble for, eat what we

can get, hungry chickens waiting
for the pot. Until one day we

slow. And straighten up. And stop.
Arguments above us, wind and money

before the roof opens, the browfow
gazing down. Our crowded faces,

empty mouths. Then they pick ten:
bones and skin hauled up, unshackled, free;

free to choose, the musket or the leap
from the lee rail into the blue below,

waiting for the breeze that soon comes,
ruffling sea-feathers, bulge and flap

of canvas, and we slant again towards
what the lookout spies days later, swaying

from his mast-top, cries of "land". Shouts
and happy gunfire, and later when the roof

opens again, this time they are pointing
at the young yarinya; Aisha, Hafsah,

me. The wind cool on my skin. Stars
scattered in the cantsee are diamonds

on black water, and in the distance, lights
as the browfow sway among us, saying

"Dance now missies, dance". Aisha first;
another one grabs Hafsah. And then me.

"Dance " he says, his breath soursweet,
and grips my arm, his one eye sharper still,

his hands all over, up and down me, up
and down until we stumble, fall. He climbs

on top, stalk hardening as he whispers "You
the sweetest, sweet as sugar sweet" and I

kick then, and kick and kick and kick,
but he's inside me, heaving hot and hard,

eyes closed, and when he stops I try
to stand, the lights ahead now brighter,

thinking of Hadi, my drowned Hadi,
and the shade of the acacia, and all around

the moans and cries of others, growing
like a dark flower in the belly of this ship.

V

The Wave

in memory of those who perished in the Fastnet Yacht Race 1979

Grizzled mainsail trimmer off a Yankee clipper
the only one to call it, cloudless August morning
in the shore-side caff. "Something big

out there in the Atlantic," southern drawl amid
Sweet Afton, waft of last night's beer, bitching
about skippers over eggs and bacon. Tinkling

masts. The gleam and spank of sail, yachts prancing
in the harbour, courses plotted for The Rock. No runic
satellite, no merry weather-man could then foretell

the mangled spars. The drifting empty hulls.
The sodden bodies hauled aboard by trawlers;
the others, never found, lists taped up in windows

near the greasy spoon where that old salt had seen
what Hokusai saw, beyond the geishas and the fishmarkets
of Edo, his own floating world as he leaned over

a wood-block carved from cherry to make his picture
of the wave off Kanagawa: out of nowhere, a rumble
in the ocean, foam-flecked surge gathering in the arc

of its own rage into a roar of water, brute beauty
trembling above the wooden sampans, the cowering men.
Poised. Ready to sweep everything away.

The Ark

Past the sign that offers WIGS FOR RENT
at Minihan's the chemist, who still complains
of rivulets of stout dribbling down into his shop;
then in under the arch through which a man might ride

a horse, and up the stairs, the same stairs Eddie Guest
once stumbled on, and fell, and sued, and lost. A door
opening into an interior by Vermeer: light falling
from a window on the left, lambent on the counter;

the figures perched on high stools nursing pints and chasers.
The sense that some small thing is just about to happen
here, where anything is possible, where merchant princes
wait their turn and Bernie Murphy, sandwich-board-man,
        becomes

a city councillor. And you, *mein host,* presiding, gazing out
across the bar at new arrivals before you amble over to pour
another splash of what you've always loved to call "a talent
to abuse", a talent nurtured in another time when *Select Bar*

meant no fools ever suffered, no interruptions tolerated to quiet,
courteous drinking. The legends grew: how once, when he refused
to remove it, you snipped off with a scissors a patron's garish tie;
how tourists seeking merely coffee or a soft drink were briskly
        shown

the door. Word was, nobody was anybody in this town
until they'd been barred by you, though at times the person
you most wanted to get rid of was yourself, your own best
        customer,
dank afternoons alone when the smoke-stained wooden panels

closed in around you like a coffin and you sank down to the
    dregs,
down to the ocean floor at the bottom of your glass. "Quit
    drinking"
said the doctor, "quit, while you're ahead". "Who says I'm
    ahead?"
the return from the baseline, proving *you can always tell a
    Corkman,*

but you can't tell him much. Some day the Lee's green waters
will rise to swallow up all of these streets; Patrick Street, and
    Winthrop,
and this street too; Oliver Plunkett, our favourite bloody
    martyr,
but when the deluge comes if anything survives it will be this
    place,

an ark filled with chairs and tables from another turn-of-century
    ship,
the picture signed by Einstein and the letter from Cole Porter,
    and forty
days and nights of classical and jazz and opera, enough even for
    you,
a balding Noah in bi-focals, still humming Shostakovich and
    insisting

on good manners as the denizens stare out upon the lost world
floating past, clinging on to Bernie Murphy's sandwich-board.

Scrimshaw

for M

Among the twisted innards, shock of crimson
he found this: a pause, mid-flense, to tuck
into the pocket of the leaky oilskin he'd

be drowned in later the little stumpy tusk,
a hundred in that fearsome head, a tooth
for every cask of viscous ooze becoming

suds lathering a widow's hands, or oil soaking
through wick, the hurricane lamp flickering
beside him, nights on deck, on watch,

boards sagging under the leviathan dead,
etching, scratching out as I do now
this story: clouds and masts, the tiny whaler

following through waves a plume of foam
engraved on this keepsake I make that you
may keep when I am all at sea, so far

from home and so much water as I
chase down the latest poem that briefly surfaces
off starboard to shouts, quivering blades

before descending once again into
the unfathomable, a deep darker than ink
or any marks I might set down tonight,

creak of moonlit rigging, the songs of long-dead
sailors carrying on a wind up from the south,
salt gust on these chapped lips that long for yours.

Crusoe, After

Listing decks. The sullen, grumbling crew
as alien as once the rustle of pimento leaves,
the waves conspiring daily with the shore,
whispering "Never, never. "Britches, shoes
long gone but some frayed thread still snags;
the island, trailing in ship's wake. At night
he gazed astern, as if a sail might loom
out of the dark again, to where he was
this time, the flames of beach-fires roaring
in his brain as bow heaved through the swell,
heading home. When she opened her legs he came
between the splayed limbs of the bower
built to shade dried goatskins, musket, Bible;
the hairy chalice of a scooped coconut shell.

Yachts, Evening

Wind dying, they are struggling
to finish, almost out of time. Is this
how it will be? My father calls me.
"Let's go sailing." One last chance
to hoist canvas before sundown,
before we put out to sea.

The Blue Man

Hulk of ferry, scream of gull; the Irish Sea
behind in darkness, shaking her grey head.
Pasty-faced in platform's sodium glare, we hefted
rucksacks and suitcases, plastic bags of duty free,

the clunk and clink of grog and cig, stashed until
engine-stammer, whistle-shriek, the rolling vowels
of Wales, train hauling its song, station after station
like the faith we'd sworn we'd keep to fearful parents

who pressed addresses into our small town hands.
Cards marked, we played brag for the new money
we jingled in our fingers, trying to weigh its sovereign
otherness; and here comes England, a man in uniform

politely clipping tickets. His velvet midnight skin; the Irish
suddenly made sense of, Miss O'Kelly at the blackboard
drumming in the word for 'negro', *an fear gorm*, the blue man
who stands before us, asking if we know where we are going.